The Portal Be (Twin) Us

OrangeBooks Publication

1st Floor, Rajhans Arcade, Mall Road, Kohka, Bhilai, Chhattisgarh 490020
Website: **www.orangebooks.in**

First Edition, 2025

ISBN: 978-93-6554-747-4

Price: Rs. 240.00

Printed in India

The Portal Be(Twin) Us

A Journey Through Resonance, Reflection, And Returning To The Real Self.

A Book By Surbhi Khandekar

OrangeBooks Publication

www.orangebooks.in

About the Book

A journey through resonance, reflection, and returning to the real self.

What if the people we meet are not coincidences, but mirrors?

This book was born from the quiet knowing that we do not simply fall in love with another person; we awaken parts of ourselves through them. The Portal Be(Twin) Us is not just a love story between two souls; it is a reminder that all relationships, especially the soul-stirring ones, are mirrors. That is when we deeply love someone, we're touching the places within us that are already love. And when we find ourselves irritated or disconnected from someone, it is often a reflection of a trait or wound we haven't yet accepted in ourselves.

We attract not what we want, but who we are. And when we truly seek someone to spend our time with, what we're longing for is often someone who thinks like us, feels like us, believes in the things we do, someone who speaks our inner language, even in silence.

So much of our life is spent looking outward for connection, companionship and validation. But the real magic happens when someone walks in and reflects our truest essence to us. When they see us not as the world does, but as we are behind the masks, beneath the roles.

In that rare resonance, healing begins. Because suddenly, we're not alone in our thoughts. We feel seen, not just admired. We feel understood, not just heard.

This is what The Portal Be(Twin) Us represents: That sacred doorway we sometimes walk through with someone…Only to find, we were walking back to ourselves all along.

Let this be a gentle reminder: If you find yourself loving someone deeply, perhaps you've finally begun to love yourself the same way. And if someone triggers discomfort, pause; they might be showing you a piece of your puzzle, waiting to be reclaimed.

After all, between us… lies the truth within us.

Foreword

What do you say about a book that doesn't just tell a story, but gently places a mirror in your hand and says: I am you, I am with you!

'The Portal Be(Twin) Us 'is not a love story in the traditional sense. It's an inward reflection. A beautiful, luminous work of awakening. A resonance. A silent recognition between two souls who were never truly strangers but just echoes of each other, meeting again in this lifetime not to complete one another, but to help each other remember who they are.

Even as children, when we barely understood the weight of words, Surbhi and I would scribble poems on torn pages and write about life as if we had lived many of them. We'd talk about energy long before we knew what vibration meant, about frequency before we'd ever heard of alignment. Our bond was always rooted in something deeper than appearances. We chose muddy fields over mirrors, NCC parades over pageantry, character over cover - up. We grew up believing that showing up real was braver than looking perfect.

Reading this book, I was reminded of those roots: the raw honesty, the thoughtful reflection, the choice to be vulnerable instead of ornamental.

The mirrored souls of this book… the co-journeyers lead of this story don't fall in love. But rise in life through their own war of thoughts, the friction, the reflection, and fragments of their past selves that were waiting to be heard. Their story is not of two halves becoming whole, but of two souls resonating at the same frequency, even in their silence. The sacred silence doesn't make either of them uncomfortable.

This book speaks about that rare, soulful connection. The kind that doesn't demand fireworks, but recognition. That quiet, steady knowing: I see you. I know you. I am you.

From the very first page, this story does not merely tell a tale; it invites you into a mirror: the one that reflects the quiet longings and unspoken truths we all carry.

In a world where love stories often revolve around dramatic rescues or perfect endings, Surbhi dares to ask a more courageous question: What if love isn't about losing ourselves to another, but about finding ourselves more fully?

Through the journey of the leads, this book tenderly unpacks the layers of conditioning that we wrap around our hearts. Rather than portraying love as something that completes us, this story reveals love as something that can awaken what already lives within us. It reminds us that two people can meet not to fix each other's cracks, but to light up the beauty in each other's imperfections.

Surbhi's writing is as soulful as it is honest. With every page, she paints moments that feel alive; the moments of hushed cafés, the scenes amidst nature carved out of childhood memories, the silences, and conversations that stay with you long after you've read the book. Her characters are flawed, real, and achingly relatable, offering not an escape from life's messiness, but a compassionate lens to see it through.

To anyone who has ever felt invisible in a crowded room, or who has yearned for a connection that transcends small talk, this book offers a gentle, powerful reminder: the most profound love story you will ever live is the one you write with yourself. Never stop loving yourself and be gentle towards your flaws. Be patient with yourself!

I am deeply proud of Surbhi's courage in writing this book, and I believe the theme of 'The Portal Be(Twin) Us 'will touch your heart as it touched mine. Two souls meet: not with fire or flame to be fed, but with a recognition of being noticed. They are not attracted physically but are inseparable spiritually. They speak in frequencies, not words. And in the pause between their sentences, their universe exhales, carrying a message to the reader that:

You were never separate, just walking the edges of the same flame. Now, you remember. Now, you return to yourself!

As her elder sister, I've had the quiet privilege of watching Surbhi grow through her own emotional and spiritual evolution. She doesn't write to impress; she writes to reveal. And this book? It's a gift. A portal. A reminder that the deepest connections often lead us not into another person's arms, but into our truth.

If you've ever sensed a bond that defied words, If you've longed for a presence that made you feel more like yourself, If you believe that love is not always loud; not always a feed to physical desires but something magical and liberating to be deeply felt, Then, 'The Portal Be(Twin) Us 'will feel like home.

Let it hold your heart gently. And let it reflect the parts of you that have been waiting to be seen. Because sometimes, the one you're searching for… is the one who helps you find yourself.

This story is an attempt to capture the beauty and hope of love that refuses to fade, even against the odds. Through these pages, I invite you to travel as the characters navigate chance encounters, meaningful silences, and moments that will change them forever. This story reminds us that love can arrive in unexpected ways, and sometimes, the greatest stories are the ones that challenge us to grow.

Thank you for picking up this book. I hope it finds you at the perfect moment in your own journey. Enjoy reading this much relatable piece of writing straight out of the heart and not just the pen.

- Sonal Sachin Gupte

(Sachisha)

Dedication

This is my first book.

A collection of reflections, resonances, and emotions that have lived inside me for years, waiting quietly to be written.

I dedicate this book to my grandfather, Mr. Gangadhar Khedekar, the first gentle soul who made me feel deeply, without needing to explain what feelings meant.

I still remember that Friday afternoon when I was in the 6th standard. I came home from school, and Ajoba handed me a 5-rupee coin." Go get a red rose for your Aaji," he said.

Confused, I looked at him and asked in Marathi, "Pan Aaji tar nahiye na?" ("But Aaji isn't here anymore, right?")

He just smiled and sent me on my way.

The rose cost three rupees. I happily kept the two-rupee change, excitedly calculating how many candies and bubble gums I could buy. Later, when I returned home, I gave him the rose, and he told me,

“Keep the change, it’s your bakshish.” I smiled widely, knowing he wouldn’t ask for it back.

I bought four candies and one Boomer gum that day.

But what I remember even more vividly is walking into his room soon after and finding him speaking softly to Aaji’s photograph. He placed the rose in front of her and whispered gently. When he saw me, he smiled and hugged me close.

“I love your Aaji very much,” he said.“ Though she’s not here anymore, I feel her around me. It’s her tithi today… she always loved red roses.”

That day, I understood that love doesn’t always end. Sometimes, it just changes form. It lives in gestures, in silences, in roses offered quietly in a room full of memories.

This book, in many ways, is that rose. Offered in love. Held in memory. And rooted in the presence of those we carry always.

Author's Note

Some stories are not written; they arrive. Softly. Slowly. Like whispers from the soul.

The Portal Be(Twin) Us was never meant to be a conventional love story. It was born from pauses between words, from the ache of silent understanding, and from those rare connections that challenge everything we thought we knew about relationships, healing, and selfhood.

Ira and Aarav were not characters I invented; they were mirrors. Reflections of all of us who've ever felt unseen in a crowd, who've longed for a deeper resonance, or who've met someone who didn't save us but simply saw us.

This story is deeply personal. Rooted in my lifelong curiosity about spiritual frequencies, soulful bonds, and the unseen energy that flows between kindred spirits. I began writing poetry at the age of 12, later wandering into travel journaling and self-reflective essays, never knowing it was leading me here.

Writing this book has been a journey of self-discovery. Certain lines echoed back to me with such intensity that I had to stop and feel them. They changed something in me. I believe they might stir something within you, too.

This book isn't about infidelity. It's not about betrayal. It's about finding your twin flame most unexpectedly, not to lose yourself, but to remember who you are. It's about the frequencies of the invisible threads that connect hearts, not through logic, but through energy, depth, and silence.

This book is for those who have loved quietly.

For those who've grown through pain.

And for anyone who has ever met someone and wondered.

"Why does it feel like I've known you before?"

As you turn the final pages, I hope you pause not for answers, but to listen to your inner portal. Because sometimes, love isn't about finding someone new… but meeting yourself, all over again.

Thank you for being here.

With love and light,

- Surbhi Khandekar

Acknowledgements

This book began as a whisper. A quiet ache between the lines of daily life, a longing to capture moments that don't always have names but live deeply within us.

To everyone who has ever felt unseen and still kept loving, this story is yours too. I extend my deepest gratitude to the people who held space for me while I poured parts of my heart into these pages.

To my grandfather, thank you for the stories, the silence, the strength. Your spirit walks with me in every word I write.

To the version of me who stayed up at night wondering, healing, and hoping, thank you for trusting the process and choosing softness, again and again.

To the ones who became mirrors in real life, reflecting things I had forgotten or never dared to look at, you've shaped this book more than you know.

I would also like to thank my husband, Mr. Vishwesh Deshmukh, for supporting me in this journey along with the little one. (Our two-year-old daughter)

To the voices that echo through this book, some imagined, some remembered, thank you for showing me that love doesn't always have to be loud. Sometimes, it's presence. Sometimes, it's resonance.

And finally, to the readers: if any part of this story felt like it was written just for you… It probably was. Thank you for opening this portal with me. May you always find your way back to yourself.

With love and deep reflection,

-Yours Surbhi

Introduction

What if love isn't something you fall into… but something you awaken within?

This is not a love story. Not in the traditional sense. This is a story of two strangers, Aarav, a quiet seeker from a small town, and Ira, a spirited soul wrapped in elegance and silence, who cross paths not by chance, but through an invisible pull of timing, frequency, and unfinished conversations with the universe.

They meet in a world full of noise, yet find solace in each other's stillness. Both trapped in relationships that look perfect on the outside but feel hollow inside, Aarav and Ira begin a journey not towards each other, but through each other.

Their connection is not rushed. There are no promises, no poetic confessions under the rain. Instead, there are pauses. Soft questions. Unfinished cups of tea. Long drives in silence. And an unspoken agreement to show up not as saviours, but as mirrors.

Through dreamlike escapes, spiritual reflections, emotional unravelling, and wild treks through real and imagined landscapes, they rediscover something far deeper than romance, their real selves.

This book invites you to explore the spaces between what is said and what is felt. To reflect on what it means to truly see and be seen. And to ask yourself the question that echoes long after the last page:

What if love is just… finally meeting yourself?

Prologue

Before the Portal Opened

There are lives that look complete from the outside, smiling faces, family photos, weekend getaways, dinner tables lit by laughter. But behind closed doors and beneath the surface, some hearts throb silently, aching for something more… something unnamed.

In two such seemingly settled lives, there existed a space neither had ever acknowledged, a void, quiet and persistent.

Aarav Verma was born in a small town in Uttar Pradesh to Kishor Verma, a disciplined government banker, and Meena Verma, a homemaker who quietly sacrificed her dreams so her son could build his. Aarav was thoughtful, observant, and often lost in his world until he met her.

Riya Ahuja.

She was in the same engineering college as Aarav, from a wealthy Sindhi family with dreams bigger than boundaries. She was confident, generous, and had a spark that ignited something within him. Aarav helped her with assignments, made notes for her, and silently cherished every moment spent together. Her presence motivated him to work harder, to finish his studies with purpose, hoping someday her parents might see him as

"Good enough."

But Riya had other plans. Midway through college, she left for an international fashion design course, chasing her ambition across oceans. Aarav missed her achingly so. They stayed in touch on and off, a fragile thread that kept pulling him back to the hope he had once built his world around.

Years later, they reunited and got married. Now living in Mumbai, Aarav and Riya have built a life together, stylish, successful, well-placed. But time has its way of showing what's missing. While Riya's world sparkled with glamour, travel, and ambition, Aarav longed for something quieter: a connection that needed no explanation.

Ira Raghav Shah, on the other hand, was raised in motion across army bases, school corridors, and echoing goodbyes. Daughter of Late Colonel Arvind Singh, a decorated army officer, and Neelam Singh, a strong and grounded schoolteacher, Ira was shaped by strength and grace in equal measure.

Her marriage was arranged through distant relatives to Raghav Shah, a third-generation Gujarati businessman from Pune. Kind, courteous, and well-settled, Raghav never stopped Ira from doing anything. He gave her freedom, expensive gifts, and planned grand holidays. But he never truly paused to understand what moved her. He didn't ask about her dreams, her thoughts, or the stories behind her silences. He never really saw her.

Ira, now settled in Pune, was content in the way society defines it. Her mother had moved there after the wedding, and she was surrounded by a few good friends. But somewhere deep inside, she missed being understood. She craved a heart-to-heart connection, a kind of emotional intimacy that no material comfort could fill.

And so, they all lived playing roles well-rehearsed. Until one day, the Universe gently turned the page.

When two souls, Aarav and Ira, met, it wasn't in rebellion. It wasn't even romantic. It was quiet, unexpected, and deeply grounding.

It wasn't love at first sight. It was recognition. A familiarity not from the past, but from something older than time.

A journey began not toward each other, but toward themselves. Through silence, messages, missed timings and mirrored emotions. A portal had opened between them one that didn't demand labels…Only truth.

Beginning before opening a Portal

The college campus bustled with late morning energy groups of students under trees with chai in hand, laughter echoing down the stone corridors, and the faint scent of chalk dust mixed with petrichor from the last night's rain.

Aarav had always walked these corridors like a quiet observer. He wasn't invisible, but he never demanded to be seen. Engineering college was a space to build a future, not an identity. Or so he thought until he saw her.

Riya Ahuja.

Hair dancing in the breeze, a careless smile on her lips, and eyes that carried stories she hadn't yet told. She wasn't trying to be noticed. She simply was vivid, unapologetic, alive.

Aarav saw her first in the library. She had walked in confidently, scanning the racks as if the books were waiting just for her. And then she sat two chairs away from him, flipping through notes that clearly weren't hers.

That was the beginning.

In the weeks that followed, they shared everything from assignment deadlines to paper - thin laughter over canteen samosas. He helped her understand circuits; she helped him understand the charm of chaos. It started with notes, grew into shared bus rides, and eventually, the kind of silences only close friends understand.

One late evening, they sat under the neem tree outside their department building. The golden light was slowly giving way to dusk. Riya had just shared something she'd been holding in for weeks.

Riya:

"I've decided. I'm applying for that design course in Milan. It's everything I've ever wanted to do."

Aarav looked at her, the ache building gently beneath his composed expression. He paused before replying.

Aarav:

"You should. You absolutely should. Dreams that big shouldn't wait. I'll miss you, Riya. But if there's one thing I know, it's that a career, a purpose that comes first."

She smiled, her eyes soft with gratitude, not pity. He wasn't holding her back. He was letting her fly.

Later that week, they sat quietly on the college rooftop. The city lights blinked below them. That's when Aarav spoke less as a friend, more as someone finally ready to say what shaped him.

Aarav:

"You know… both of us are the only children of our respective parents. So, we carry a bit more weight than we talk about. Expectations. Loneliness. Pressure to be everything." (He glanced away for a moment, then continued.)" My father… he had nothing growing up. But he built a name for himself in banking. That took us to better places, big towns, even Delhi for a while. But the journey, the grind… it wasn't just his."

He grew quieter.

Aarav (softly):

"My mother, Meena she followed silently. She left everything she once wanted. She found joy in raising me, yes. But somewhere along the way, I think she lost herself." (A pause. His voice cracks almost imperceptibly.)" She tells me often make something of yourself, but don't lose yourself in the process. She says it like a whisper. As if she's saying it to herself, too."

He fell silent. A long silence. His mind wandered into a memory he didn't share.

Riya looked at him with a new depth in her eyes, not as the boy who helped her with circuits, but as someone carrying invisible weights with grace.

Riya (gently):

"I understand, Aarav."

And just like that, the moment broke. From the basketball court nearby, someone shouted her name.

"Riyaaaa! Come fast! You'll miss the bet!"

She rolled her eyes playfully, gave Aarav a light pat on his shoulder.

Riya (smiling):

"Duty calls. Some bet about who can eat five Vada pavs without water, don't ask."

She laughed and ran off, her voice blending into the fading light. Aarav watched her go, a half-smile tugging at his lips.

Then, without a word, he turned and walked back to the library, the place where it had all begun, and perhaps, where something within him had quietly changed.

(A few years later)

Somewhere in Ira's life: Companionship is more than just promises

The afternoon sun filtered softly through the sheer curtains of Ira's Pune bungalow. The living room was filled with quiet warmth. Neelam Singh, Ira's mother, sat comfortably on the sofa, lost in the pages of a well-worn novel, her reading glasses slipping down her nose. The only sound was the gentle clink of a teacup being placed on the side table.

In the study down the hall, Ira sat at her desk, her pen moving thoughtfully across the pages of her journal. The silence was her sanctuary, a space where she could untangle the thoughts that rarely found space in spoken words.

Just then, the soft knock of the maid interrupted her rhythm.

Maid (gently):

"Didi… Priya madam aayi hai. Unke saath unka fiancé bhi hai."

Ira blinked, surprised but pleased. She tucked the pen into her notebook and stood, smoothing the folds of her kurta. As she stepped into the living room, she saw Priya, her college friend, radiant as ever, standing beside her fiancé, Aniruddh, polite, well-dressed, and visibly a little nervous.

A warm smile crossed Ira's face as she approached them.

Ira

"Priya… you look beautiful. I'm truly happy for both of you."

(She turned toward Aniruddh, with gentle eyes and a kind smile.)

"Aniruddh, I don't know you yet, but I hope you won't mind a little advice from someone who's seen a bit of life."

She paused just enough to let her words settle, her voice soft yet steady.

Ira

"Only go ahead when your souls feel connected, not just your lives. I'm not complaining, truly… I have everything one could ask for. Raghav has given me a beautiful life, freedom, respect, and even luxuries I never imagined. And yet…" (She looked away for a moment, almost to herself.)" I find myself missing the feeling of being seen. Not just looked at but truly understood."

The room grew quieter, the moment gently tender. Her mother looked up briefly from her book, eyes calm but knowing. Priya reached out and held Ira's hand, saying nothing, but hearing everything.

Priya (softly):

"Ira… you've always had the courage to speak the truth, your truth. Most of us spend our lives adjusting to what looks good on the outside. But you… You remind me that there's something deeper we should all be paying attention to." (She glanced at Aniruddh, then back at Ira.)" And maybe that's what scares me a little. I love him… I think I do. But do we see each other completely yet? I don't know."

Aniruddh shifted slightly but said nothing. It wasn't discomfort, it was reflection. The silence between them wasn't awkward. It was honest.

Just then, Neelam ji placed a bookmark between the pages of her novel and spoke, her voice calm, with the weight of years behind it.

Neelam Singh:" Every marriage begins with hopes, not guarantees. The question is, do you enter it with awareness or with a blindfold? When I married your father, we were strangers. But we made the effort to look into each other, not just across." (She looked at Ira with quiet affection.)" I see my daughter still making that effort, even when the world says she has everything. That's what makes her rare."

Ira lowered her eyes, both grateful and emotional.

Ira (softly)

"Maybe we all just want to be met not halfway, but deeply."

The wind stirred the curtains gently. Outside, the Gul Mohar trees stood still in the sun. Inside, something invisible had shifted a moment of reflection shared between women, each standing at a different edge of love.

The Return

Four years had passed, but it felt like a lifetime.

The Mumbai skyline shimmered through the floor-to-ceiling windows of Aarav's apartment, sleek, modern, and meticulously put together. Much like the man who now stood before the mirror, adjusting his cufflinks.

Aarav Verma, 28 now, was no longer the boy from the engineering corridors. He had grown into a sharp, dashing gentleman disciplined, well-travelled, and quietly magnetic. After working across major cities in India and handling projects in New York, Seattle, and San Francisco, he had carved a space for himself in the corporate world. Promotions had come, respect had followed, and money had started flowing with ease.

His apartment in a prime Mumbai neighbourhood was a silent testament to years of hard work, walnut wood, textured grey walls, subtle art, and books he still read by the window.

But that morning, there was something different in the air. He was flying to Delhi not for work, but for something… familiar. To pick her up.

Riya Ahuja.

The name still carried weight in his chest, though he'd carefully placed it in the quiet corners of his life all these years.

Her course in Milan had gone longer than expected extended internships, travel, and design exhibitions. Their conversations had reduced to annual birthday texts and occasional "hope you're doing well" emails.

And now, she was coming back.

At Delhi Airport.

Aarav stood at Arrivals, tall and calm in a navy-blue shirt tucked neatly into tailored chinos. He checked his watch out of habit, even though the flight had landed. The automatic doors slid open, and streams of passengers began to trickle out.

And then he saw her.

Riya.

Her hair had changed, now a deep caramel brown with soft waves framing her face. She wore a long trench coat over a black crop top and high-waisted jeans, effortlessly chic, confidently poised. Her eyes scanned the crowd, and when they found his, they sparkled with recognition. She walked toward him with the same familiar easc, but something about her had undeniably shifted.

She was still Riya but layered with Europe, independence, and something sharper… maybe solitude.

Aarav felt something stir. Not just attraction but a quiet awe.

Riya (smiling):

"Aarav Verma… look at you! If I didn't know better, I'd think you've stepped out of a Vogue office."

He laughed softly, still taking her in.

Aarav:

"And you… Italy loved you."

She twirled once with playful pride.

Riya:

"And I loved it back. But it's good to be home."

As they walked toward the parking lot, the initial laughter softened. The air between them carried memories, unspoken questions, and a certain inevitability.

Aarav opened the car door for her, his sleek black SUV reflecting a version of himself she had never seen before.

Inside the car, as Delhi passed by outside the tinted windows, Aarav caught himself stealing glances at her. She was so different, and yet so deeply familiar. The girl he once tutored, laughed with under neem trees, and watched disappear through the departure gate was now here beside him, glowing in her light.

And deep inside, a voice whispered:“ She’s the reason you worked so hard… why you built all this… why you became more.”

By the time they reached his parents ’house, where Kishor and Meena Verma had now settled post-retirement, the first signs of the past merging with the present began to show. Familiar conversations turned into long walks. Smiles lingered longer. His mother noticed. His father said little, but observed everything.

Within a few days, marriage talks began first lightheartedly, then with more intention. Friends and families rekindled connections. Even Aarav’s old house in their hometown was cleaned up, as if some part of the past wanted to witness what the future held.

But something within Aarav had changed, too. He wasn't chasing her this time. He had become someone he was proud of. And yet… he wondered silently:

Did they still see each other the same way? Or had time crafted two different versions of love?

Doubt about wedding bells.

The courtyard of the Verma house in Delhi carried a stillness that belonged to quiet mornings. The bougainvillaea vines curled gently around the railings, and the scent of cardamom chai lingered in the air.

Meena Verma sat cross-legged on the verandah swing, the same one where she used to rock baby Aarav to sleep. Her greying hair was tied in a loose braid, her cotton saree creased in the way that comes only from long hours of comfort. A book lay open on her lap, but her eyes weren't on the words.

They were on her son standing by the tulsi plant, staring out at nothing, holding a cup of tea that had long stopped steaming.

She smiled to herself. She knew this stillness in him. It always came before his storms of thought.

Meena (softly):

"She's lovely. Confident. Polished. The world has kissed her with experiences most of us only read about."

Aarav looked at his mother, slightly startled, then smiled. She always knew what he was thinking. Sometimes, before even he did.

Aarav

"She's changed… but in a good way. And yet, I don't know why I feel this… quiet distance."

Meena patted the space beside her. Aarav walked over and sat down. The swing creaked gently beneath their shared silence.

Meena:

"Aarav, when you were a boy, you once told me you would become so successful that no one would ever question your worth. And now, here you are successful, kind, settled." (She looked at him gently.)" But that old dream… was it for you? Or for someone else?"

Aarav looked away; the rim of the teacup pressed lightly to his lips.

Meena (continued):

"I see how you look at her, and I see how you hold back, too. It's okay, beta. Not every love story must continue just because it once began. Sometimes… people grow in different directions, and that's not failure. That's life."

Aarav swallowed the knot in his throat. The honesty was disarming.

Aarav (softly):

"I did all this thinking of her. That maybe if I became more, she'd come back and stay. But now that she's here, I wonder if she's still the girl I once knew or if I've changed too much to belong in the same chapter."

Meena placed her hand over his.

Meena:

"The girl you loved inspired you. But the man you've become is your own doing. And that matters. If you both still choose each other, do it as the people you are now. Not as a reward for the journey you've already crossed."

Just then, a faint voice echoed from inside.

" Aarav, Riya's looking for you!"

He looked back once more at his mother.

Meena (smiling):

"Go talk to her. But don't forget, no one else can give you your identity, beta. You already built it. Now ask yourself… do you want to share it with her?"

Aarav stood slowly, kissed his mother's forehead, and walked back inside.

Somewhere deep inside, the boy who once wanted to be seen was beginning to see himself clearly, for the very first time.

A story of unseen threads, healing souls, and timeless connection.

Content

Chapter - 1

Parallel Lives

"Sometimes, two people live miles apart, but their hearts breathe the same silence."

Aarav – The Filtered Man

The sound of a toothbrush being dropped into a mug echoed through the empty bathroom. Aarav looked into the mirror, face half-shaved, the other half lost in thought. His eyes, once curious, now carried the weariness of quiet survival.

He stepped into the bedroom, pulling his formal shirt over his shoulders. The sky outside was blue, too blue for how heavy his chest felt.

Sunlight streamed through the half-open blinds, landing on a dusty corner of the drawer he rarely touched. Out of some inexplicable instinct, he opened it.

Files, warranties, corporate IDs… medals from school debates and college elocutions. He hadn't looked at these in years.

And then, beneath a faded envelope, he found his old diary. The cover had peeled, but inside were pages of ink-stained thoughts from a version of him that felt… alive.

He smiled wryly." God, I used to feel so much," he whispered, flipping through a few pages.

His wife, Riya, called out from the living room, "You'll be late, Aarav. "

"Coming," he replied, voice neutral, almost practised.

As he left the room, the diary lay open behind him like a quiet protest.

Office Chaos & Silent Longing

The constant clatter of keyboards and buzzing phones filled the air as Aarav sat inside his glass-walled cabin. Spreadsheets blinked on his screen, notifications piled on the corner, and yet his eyes remained unfocused. The office outside was alive in its chaotic rhythm.

He rose, instinctively straightening his shirt as he stepped out.

A colleague leaned against the coffee machine, laughing, with a latte in hand, while two others whispered near the printer, their brows knitted over an unfixable client mess. A young intern was pacing in the corridor, phone pressed to his ear, gesturing as if urgency alone would fix everything.

Aarav stood still amidst the movement.

The hallway hummed with voices, footsteps, a door shutting somewhere, a printer coughing paper. But inside him, it was stillness mixed with noise. Thoughts collided with unfinished dreams, childhood notebooks filled with poetry, guitar strings now rusting in a forgotten corner, and the ache of constantly proving his worth.

“Is this it?”

“Is this what I worked so hard for?

“Deadlines. Metrics. Expectations. Repeat.”

He walked over to the vending machine, fingers moving on autopilot, collecting the paper cup of lukewarm coffee. The bitter smell grounded him briefly.

With quiet steps, he made his way to the balcony connected to his cabin, the only space that felt untouched by the buzz. The sky stretched above like an open canvas. A group of birds darted across it, fluid, free, unbothered. The wind brushed his shirt gently, as if whispering what he had forgotten.

He leaned on the railing, cup in hand, his breath slowing." They don't worry about achievements. They just fly," he thought." They just... are."

And then a knock. Aarav turned slightly, pulled from his thought.

Vedant stood at the doorway, holding a folder and a nervous smile." Sorry, Aarav. Got two minutes?"

Aarav nodded, one last glance toward the sky. He walked back in, carrying the scent of stillness with him.

Chaos, Laughter & a Dhaba Night

As Vedant stepped into Aarav's cabin holding a folder, he noticed Aarav's faraway expression and chuckled.

"Boss, are you meditating with your eyes open now?" Vedant joked, tossing the file on the desk.

Aarav gave a half-smile. "Just zoning out. Too much noise around."

Vedant plopped onto the visitor's chair. "Know what you need? A bike ride to Lonavala. Wind in your face, no emails chasing you, just chai, Vada pav, and a rain-soaked highway. I went last weekend. Got drenched like a filmy hero. I swear, even the potholes felt romantic!"

Aarav laughed a real one. The kind that surprised even him.

"You know what?" he said, standing up and stretching. "I'm not in the mood to go home by car. Ask the driver to return the car. I'll come with you."

Vedant raised an eyebrow. "Whoa. Who are you and what have you done to our Aarav? "

"Shut up and drive," Aarav said with a smirk.

The car moved out of the corporate district into a livelier part of the city. Neon signs blurred past the windows. The monotony of files and suits slowly melted into honks, roadside stalls, kids chasing balloons, and the scent of roasting corn.

"Stop here," Aarav said suddenly, rolling up his sleeves.

Vedant looked confused. "At a dhaba? "

"Yes. I need food that tastes like home and a place where no one cares how I hold my spoon."

They sat cross-legged on plastic chairs, sharing hot parathas, dal tadka, and a steel jug of chaas. Aarav looked around families laughing, uncles yelling across tables, kids feeding each other messily. No filters. No airs.

He smiled quietly.

"Money can buy dinners, but this… this joy is homemade," he thought." It's in not caring. It's in people. It's in peeling the formality off your skin."

Vedant was halfway into a story about how he almost got chased by monkeys during a hike, and Aarav laughed so hard that his eyes watered.

Later that night, in a corner of his apartment lit only by a standing lamp, Aarav opened his laptop.

Corporate life gave him money. But words? Words gave him breath.

He logged into his favourite writing portal, a semi-private blog space where people wrote about inner work, trauma healing, and manifestations. No selfies, no bios, just real talk.

His user handle: ***@wildmind88***

He began typing.

"Sometimes, I miss myself more than I miss people…"

In the second post, he posted:

"Today felt like a desi detox. Parathas, silly jokes, no dress code, and not once did I feel the pressure to be someone.

A dhaba, a dusty highway, and laughter without purpose. The day spent well in desi style. 🛵 🌿

Turns out, peace sometimes wears chappals and smells like tadka.

@wildmind88"

That night, while she was sitting in her room's balcony, legs folded on a thin mattress, fairy lights glowing dimly above her, and a cup of masala chai resting beside her journal, Ira scrolled gently through the portal.

Outside, the city buzzed faintly. But up here, everything felt still.

Her eyes paused on a fresh post.

@wildmind88:

The day spent well in desi style. 🛵 🌿

She read it once, then again, like the words were humming something she had forgotten.

Within minutes of posting, a notification popped. A comment from an Unknown user: @BareSoulLetters: "Maybe because people never gave you back to yourself."

She replied to his first post:

Sometimes, I miss myself more than I miss people…”

He paused.

That hit hard.

She didn’t know the person behind the post, not really. But it reminded her of something that had been missing from her own life. Something uncomplicated. Warm. Lived.

She smiled softly and didn’t hit like or comment. Instead, she pulled her knees closer, sipped her tea, and opened her thoughts to the portal.

She posted again indirectly to convey **@wildmind88**.

@baresoulletters :

“Everyone’s crazy about pizzas and pastas…

But give me spicy pani puri on a rainy street any day. Fingers messy, nose running, eyes watering… and heart smiling.

Somehow, that chaos feels more like me. 🌧□🍃🌶□”

She posted it, placed her phone aside, and closed her eyes for a moment, letting the night breeze tangle her thoughts.

When she returned to her screen, a soft notification blinked:

@wildmind88 liked your post.

Her heart skipped not in excitement, but in an odd feeling of being noticed. Felt. Echoed.

“He doesn’t know me,” she thought, “but why does it feel like he just did?”

In that balcony, lit by dim lights and dreams, she sat in silence not alone, but somehow… accompanied.

Ira – The Fire in the Breeze

The other day, Sunlight spilt across her living room like soft gold. Ira sat cross-legged on the floor near the window, one hand stirring her chai absently, the other scrolling through a document draft.

A small glass jar of water stood nearby her indoor plant, a pathos, dipped its roots inside.

She took a sip, made a face.“ Too much ginger,” she muttered, then chuckled. “Just like me extra.”

Her husband Raghav was already gone for the day. Their schedules rarely aligned, and when they did, conversations were limited to grocery lists or muted dinner table small talk.

She leaned back against the wall. Outside, the city was rushing. Inside her? Stillness… and maybe, just maybe, the quiet thrill of being seen.

She thought about how corporate life had sucked the colour out of her. Her boss had praised her until she outshone him, then quietly sidelined her.

So, she'd quit. Not dramatically. Not with fireworks. Just… left. And started writing full-time.

Here on the portal, she was raw, honest, quirky, and unfiltered. Here, she was her.

Parallel Echoes

In two different homes, two different cities, under two separate skies, Aarav and Ira continued their routines.

She watered her plants and made playlists of old Hindi songs and indie tracks. He worked through meetings with a poker face, replying to messages with 🙏 and 🙂.

But come nightfall, they returned to the portal. Not just to post but to listen.

There was something electric, something intimate, about being known through your words, and not your face.

They didn't know each other's names. But they knew each other's silences.

The Quiet Between Us.

Time, as always, did what it does best: it moved forward, without asking.

A year after Riya returned from Milan, they got engaged. There was celebration, laughter, and a sense of things falling into place. Two families, two cities, one story that finally made it to the surface.

They married the following spring under fairy lights and orchid arches. Riya in an ivory lehenga, Aarav in a deep pearl white sherwani. Friends said they looked like a dream. Even Aarav believed it that day.

Now, it was their third anniversary. On paper, everything was beautiful.

Aarav had risen to a senior role at his firm, often flying out for global summits and client pitches. His hard work had finally paid off. Riya, too, had built something powerful, her designer label, now worn by celebrities and influencers alike. Her face was often seen in glossies, her work praised on talk shows. She travelled frequently, flitting between Delhi, Mumbai, and fashion hubs like Paris and Dubai.

They were married. They loved each other. They had built what everyone would call "a good life."

And yet…

One fine evening, cruising at 38,000 feet above sea level, Aarav sat by the window of his flight from

Dubai to Mumbai, staring out at the endless dusk painted across the clouds. The afterglow of the city lights far below mirrored something in his eyes, flickering, distant, unreachable.

His reflection in the glass stared back at him.

Well-groomed. Successful. Married. Settled. And yet… not entirely seen.

He touched the glass softly, as if trying to feel the person on the other side.

Aarav (whispering to himself):

" Is this it? Is this what life is supposed to feel like?"

" Is this… what love is?"

He didn't doubt his love for Riya. But something within felt misplaced. As if he'd been walking in perfectly polished shoes that never really fit.

The thought passed quietly as the captain announced descent. Aarav reached into his bag, pulling out the anniversary gift he had picked for Riya: a limited-edition designer watch from Dubai, elegant and expensive. He smiled faintly. She'd love it. But the smile didn't quite reach his eyes.

That night, back home in Mumbai, dinner was quiet but warm. Riya was dressed effortlessly in one of her creations, her phone lighting up occasionally with messages from stylists and clients. They exchanged gifts, a quick kiss, and a few laughs. They even cut a small cake.

But once the house dimmed, and the city fell silent, Aarav retreated to his study, the one corner of the house untouched by polish. He sat there in his shirt sleeves, sipping cold coffee that had gone bitter with time.

Out of habit or maybe instinct, he opened his laptop. Tired of corporate dashboards and daily briefs, he clicked on a random blog portal he hadn't visited in years. It was filled with reflections, thoughts, and anonymous stories.

That's when something caught his eye.

A *post titled:*

" To be understood without having to explain that is love."

Written by someone under the name: **@baresoulletters**

The words were simple, yet they struck a quiet place within him. He read more about silent longings, spiritual reflections, emotional frequency, and the ache of feeling everything while showing nothing.

Without thinking much, Aarav clicked 'Like'.

Then, slowly, he created his anonymous profile:

@wildmind88

That night, his first post:

"Sometimes I wonder if I've built a beautiful cage and called it home."

He didn't know who @baresoulletters was.

But her words felt like conversations he had with himself in silence.

There was no intention, no plan. Just resonance.

And in the stillness of his study, Aarav didn't realise that the portal he had just entered wasn't just digital. It was emotional. And it had only just begun.

A few days later somewhere in Europe, but Far From Each Other

It was meant to be a break from deadlines, from distractions, from the weight of routine. Aarav had been silently craving stillness. Not just the absence of work, but the presence of connection. The kind where two people pause long enough to really look at each other. So, when Riya suggested a holiday, he had said yes, hoping Europe would be more than just a destination maybe it would be a reunion.

But from the very first day, it was clear they were travelling together, yet not journeying as one.

Riya had meticulously planned a glamorous itinerary branded shopping streets in Milan, rooftop restaurants in Paris, and picture-perfect alleys of Santorini. Each day felt like a photoshoot. Each location, a backdrop. Her suitcase unpacked into layers of designer clothes, accessories colour-coded to locations, shoes for breakfast, lunch, and dinner.

Aarav had imagined long conversations over warm bread and coffee in quiet cafés.

Instead, she was on video calls showing outfits, sharing views, capturing moments in frames, but not living in them.

He watched her laugh through screens, pose for strangers, and fix her lipstick before the next photo. She was happy, in her way. But not with him.

He had become the man holding the phone, not her hand.

One afternoon, while she scrolled through filters deciding which picture to post next, Aarav sat alone at a café corner, sipping a lukewarm espresso, watching the world pass by. And it hit him not in anger, not in drama, but in quiet clarity.

He didn't need luxury.

He didn't need picture-perfect moments.

He just needed presence.

If you're truly connected with someone, he thought, you can sit on a broken bench near a chai tapri, share silence, and still feel full. You lose sense of time, not patience.

But when the connection fades when souls drift even in the most beautiful places, you feel invisible.

Riya returned to the table, still mid-call, laughing about something he wasn't a part of. She didn't notice the untouched coffee. Or the distant look in his eyes.

And that's when Aarav realised he hadn't come on this trip just for sightseeing. He came hoping to find them again.

But sometimes, when you travel too far outward, you forget how to travel inward. And love becomes just another passport stamp, beautiful in pictures, but empty in memory.

"They (Aarav and Ira) hadn't met, hadn't spoken, hadn't even shared a real photo. But somehow, their words curled into each other like warm threads in winter. Not love. Not yet. But something softer... something sacred."

Chapter - 2

The Portal of Words

"You can fall in love with someone's mind long before you meet their eyes."

Night Scrolls & Quiet Sparks

Aarav lay on the balcony floor that night, wrapped in a thin blanket, headphones in, playing an old Prateek Kuhad playlist on loop. The city skyline blinked in silence.

His laptop rested on his chest, warm and comforting. He refreshed the portal.

New comment.

@baresoulletters: "What do you miss most about yourself?"

He stared at the screen for a long minute before typing:

@wildmind88: "I miss laughing at silly things. I miss dancing while brushing my teeth. I miss not worrying if someone's watching."

And then he hesitated… but added:

"You ask questions like you've met my shadow before."

Miles away, Ira smiled at her screen. She had just curled up in her favourite armchair with a cup of chamomile tea, her fairy lights casting a soft hue on the walls.

Her fingers hovered before she typed:

@baresoulletters: "Maybe your shadow and mine go on secret walks when we sleep."

She clicked send and chuckled softly.

"This is wild," she whispered to herself.

The Comfort of Being Unseen

Over the next few days, their online interaction grew quietly, deeply. No flirting, no emojis, no pressure. Just words that felt like safe spaces.

@wildmind88:

"Ever feel like you're performing in your own life?"

@baresoulletters:

"Every single day. But then I come here and take off the costume."

They began timing their posts almost unintentionally, both showing up around 10 PM, like two lanterns lighting up the same part of the digital sky.

Sometimes, their conversations lasted hours. Sometimes, just one sentence was enough.

Post Europe trip, A week later

Gram book Post by **@wildmind88**

📷 A black-and-white picture of an empty bench by a quiet roadside tea stall. A used clay cup on the side table, an untouched second cup beside it.

Caption:

Sometimes, it's not the places that leave you exhausted…

It's the effort to feel seen while being right next to someone.

Europe had everything: castles, cafés, and colours…

But no connection.

And then you realise A chai tapri, a simple silence, and someone who truly sees you…that's the real luxury.

#Wildthoughts #thepresencegap #quietrealizations #soultravel

Comment by **@baresoulletters** (Ira)

You just put into words what I couldn't even explain to myself last week.

There was music, lights, a crowd. I wore a smile. Held the glass. But when a man asked me to dance after handing me a second drink, I looked across the room for the one person who was supposed to notice I wasn't okay. Instead, he looked away.

Sometimes you aren't hurt by strangers. You're hurt by the one who was supposed to protect your quiet "No". (Aarav didn't find it appropriate to ask at that moment.)

Flashback: Somewhere away, A Day in Ira's life

A Private Gathering at a Business Party

The lights were soft but artificial, dimmed just enough to cast a glow of elegance across the rooftop. The air was buzzing with expensive perfumes, clinking glasses, and surface-level laughter. Raghav moved through the crowd effortlessly, shaking hands, making introductions, every gesture smooth, every smile calculated.

Ira stood near the corner of the open bar, holding a glass of wine she hadn't asked for but took out of courtesy when Raghav handed it to her. She swirled it more than she sipped it, her eyes scanning the crowd, already feeling misplaced.

Earlier that evening, they had disagreed over something small but revealing." What do you want to eat later?" she had asked, scrolling through options of local food joints that served simple comfort meals." Ira, we're going to a five-star event. You don't eat street food after that." "It's not about the place, Raghav. It's about the mood, the craving." He had already moved on, barely registering her words.

They were different, she felt it more tonight than ever before. She was the kind of woman who could light up a room with her laughter, dance freely under fairy lights, and eat from food trucks at midnight without caring who watched. She didn't need luxury, she needed connection.

But this party wasn't hers.

It was Raghav's world, curated, controlled, business-class connections where smiles were transactions and relationships were leverage.

She noticed it the moment one of Raghav's senior associates, a well-dressed man with an ageing charm and overconfident tone, approached her. He refilled her glass without asking and leaned in with a smirk, "Come, Ira. One dance won't hurt."

She stepped back, her polite smile tightening." I'm good, thank you."

Across the room, she met Raghav's eyes. He gestured slightly, as if nudging her to go along. As if her discomfort was less important than keeping the guest entertained.

Her heart sank. In that one moment, it all became clear.

Raghav wasn't seeing her.

He was seeing a woman who should fit in with his lifestyle, perform, please, blend.

But Ira didn't want to blend.

Later, on the drive back, silence sat between them like a third person.

"You didn't have to make it awkward, Ira," Raghav finally said.

She looked at him calmly, voice steady." I wasn't awkward. I was uncomfortable. There's a difference."

He scoffed. "It was just a drink and a dance. "

"No, Raghav. It wasn't just a drink. I took the first glass from him because I respect you. But when someone else poured it again, without asking, you should have protected my space, not expected me to perform."

He didn't respond. She turned her gaze to the window, city lights blurring as her thoughts grew clearer.

In that moment, Ira didn't just feel the distance between them. She understood it. He built his life around business. She was learning to build hers around boundaries.

She couldn't say anything about it that day. She went into her memories and logged out, thinking about the unknown man behind the portal.

A Familiar Stranger

The soft hum of wind chimes floated through the open windows of Ira's house. The evening had settled in with a dusky lavender hue. A half-burnt sandalwood vanilla candle flickered on her writing desk, casting dancing shadows on the wall.

Ira sat on her floor mattress, her hair tied in a messy bun, wearing an old lilac sweatshirt that smelled faintly of Chanel's perfume and ink. The world outside was moving book festivals, home décore exhibitions, Raghav's client dinners, but her inner world had slowed down lately. Not in sadness, just… stillness.

She sipped her herbal tea and opened her laptop, logging into the portal where she shared her writings under the name @baresoulletters. For the world, she was a graceful, articulate woman. For this portal, she was raw, wordless, open. Here, she didn't write to impress. She wrote to survive.

Her last post had done surprisingly well:" To be understood without having to explain that is love."

She scrolled past dozens of comments, kind words, poetic responses, and then paused.

A new follower.

Handle: @wildmind88

Intrigued by the name, she clicked.

There was only one post that day. Simple. Undramatic. Yet it left her heart strangely stirred.

"Sometimes I wonder if I've built a beautiful cage and called it home."

She read it again.

And again.

There was something about the way the sentence was structured. Not dramatic. Honest. Familiar. As if someone else had also been journaling quietly into the night with no one to read them but the walls.

She clicked follow back. Not out of curiosity, but resonance.

Something in her stirred not attraction, not fantasy. Just recognition.

Like two souls whispering the same poem in different rooms.

She didn't write anything in response. But she sat quietly for a while, her tea now cold, fingers grazing the keys of her laptop. Then she opened a blank page and typed:

"There are people we never meet, but our silence aligns like constellations. Maybe healing doesn't always come from knowing names, but from recognising frequencies."

She didn't post it yet. Just saved it in drafts.

Outside, the wind rustled the leaves. Inside, two souls miles apart had brushed ever so gently against each other.

Neither of them knew yet. But something unnamed had begun to bloom in the unspoken words.

One night, Aarav asked:

"Why do your words feel like home?"

Ira stared at the screen, heart thudding gently. She typed, then deleted. Typed again.

Finally, she sent:

"Because they come from someone who had to build their own."

Real Lives, Real Weight

By day, Ira was navigating client calls for her freelance writing projects, helping her mother-in-law choose curtains, answering Raghav's occasional texts about weekend plans.

But at night, she bloomed. Her writings were messier, bolder, more vulnerable. She began opening up about childhood, how being a 'good girl 'always meant being quiet, being agreeable, being… small.

Aarav read every word like it was a letter written to him.

He, too, started writing more personally about how achieving financial security didn't fill the void, about how being "husband material" wasn't the same as being seen.

DM Chat (Private Chat Box)

And Aarav dared to DM her. If you don't mind, can I ask you something?

Ira:

read (hesitated) Replied: okay Aarav:

What happened that day? You suddenly logged off?

Ira:

started typing (In hesitation and felt sharing it with a stranger.)

Aarav:

I read your comment thrice.

That "quiet no" hit hard.

Ira:

It was loud inside me. But invisible to him.

Aarav: (Aarav talking about his trip to Europe with Riya)

I get that. With Riya, everything was captured except us. It felt like I was just a silhouette in her curated life.

Ira:

It's strange, isn't it?

How two people can be in the same place, same room, same photo…And still feel like parallel lives.

Aarav:

Exactly.

It's like… you're physically there, but emotionally ghosted.

Ira:

I don't want to live in scenes where I'm just background music in someone else's highlight reel.

Aarav:

You deserve to be the moment, not just part of the aesthetic.

Ira:

And you deserve to have your chai heard. Not just held. I hope someday someone sits with you in silence and it feels like music.

Aarav:

And I hope someone sees the power in your soft no…and never lets it go unheard again.

Ira:

I needed this chat more than I thought.

Aarav:

Me too.

Sometimes, healing doesn't come from fixing the moment.

It comes from being understood afterwards.

Ira:

I don't know why, but our conversations feel like pauses in a fast-forward life. Like a place I can finally breathe.

Aarav:

Maybe that's what connection is.

Ira:

No effort. No pretending. Just space. It's rare. And I don't take it for granted.

Aarav:

Same.

We've been typing too much lately. It would be nice to not text for once, and just talk.

Ira:

Over chai? Not in Europe this time, I hope 😄

Aarav:

No fancy cities. No itinerary. Just one quiet place. You and I. A little detour from life.

Ira:

Sounds tempting. I could use a detour. Maybe the universe is already plotting a chai plan for us.

Aarav:

Wouldn't surprise me. It always seems to find a way to bring us to the same frequency.

Ira:

If you find a spot you know, the kind where the chai is strong and the silence isn't awkward send me a pin drop.

Aarav:

Deal.

And you bring the journal. I'll bring the pause.

Ira:

Done.

Let's meet where the noise ends and the real begins.

The Voice Note

One night, a bold idea occurred to Ira.

She recorded a short voice note.

"Hi. This probably breaks the whole 'no names, no voices 'vibe, but… I just wanted to say, your words have helped me sleep on days my anxiety refused to. So… thank you. That's it. Goodnight."

She almost didn't send it. But something in her said he needed to hear that.

When Aarav opened the message the next morning, he sat still for minutes.

It wasn't the voice itself; it was how real it felt. Not performative. Not curated. Just… warm.

He replied with a text:

"That's the kindest goodnight I've heard in years."

And then:

"Maybe next time, I'll send a voice note too. But only if you promise not to ghost me if I sound like a tired corporate zombie."

She laughed out loud, alone in her kitchen.

He was funny. And real. And becoming part of her day without trying.

"They hadn't exchanged names yet nor shared pictures. But somehow, they were already more real to each other than most people they saw every day."

Chapter - 3

Almost Met

"Some souls orbit each other like stars close enough to feel, but not ready to touch."

Aarav - The Boy Who Grew Up Filtering Himself

It was raining the day Aarav got promoted.

The office clapped politely, his manager offered a firm handshake, and someone cracked a joke about him finally being "management matériel." Aarav smiled, nodded, and thanked them all.

But the real applause echoed in his head in his father's voice.

"When you stand on your own feet, only then do you deserve a seat at the table."

His father had worked as a government banker for 34 years in a small town in Uttar Pradesh. A man of routines and savings, who rarely smiled but always showed up. Aarav had grown up watching him carry the weight of stability like an iron briefcase.

His mother, Meena, was the quiet sun of the house. Her dreams lived in the faded stitching of old saris and the scent of books she never had time to read. She had taught herself English just to help Aarav with school projects.

Once, as a teenager, he'd asked," Ma, didn't you want to work?"

She'd smiled softly, placing a steel plate in front of him.

"Beta, some of us choose to be the soil so someone else can bloom."

That line never left him. It haunted him, especially now when he had bloomed, but felt rootless.

Ira – The Girl Made of Cities and Silences

Ira scribbled in her journal with a blue gel pen, the kind she'd always borrowed from her army dad's uniform pocket.

"Today, the wind sounds like Leh at 6 a.m. Cold, honest, and wild."

Her house in Pune overlooked a quiet park. A squirrel darted across the balcony railing, and the sunlight shimmered through her chimes, casting shifting shadows across the room.

She had always felt places deeply like people.

Maybe it was because she'd grown up everywhere: Shenlong, Coimbatore, Jaipur, Kochi, Kashmir. Every two years, a new school. A new dialect. A new set of girls who already had their best friends.

Her father, Colonel Arvind Singh, had once shown her the stars on a clear night in Ladakh and said,

"Always know where you are. Longitude. Latitude. Not just on the map in life."

He was killed during a counter-terror operation when she was seventeen. Since then, her mother had become her storm and shelter, both tough as steel, never once letting Ira see her break.

Mirror Conversations between Ira and Aarav

That night, as the city glowed like embers under twilight, Ira posted:

"What if our grief is coded into the places we've been? Maybe that's why we revisit them, hoping memory will turn into meaning."

Aarav replied instantly:

@wildmind88:

"I was just thinking today how I miss the smell of damp earth after summer rain. Maybe because that's where I buried my softest versions."

She smiled. She could feel him even without seeing him.

Later, during their usual 10 p.m. chat, she sent a voice note:

"You know, sometimes I wish I had a sibling to share this weird mix of memory and madness with. But maybe that's why I write, I split myself into parts so someone can read and say, 'me too.'"

Aarav chuckled as he played it.

He replied in text:

"Same here. I used to imagine a twin brother who'd take the fall when I broke something or forgot homework. I think we're all just writing to siblings we never had."

The Almost Plan

They almost planned to meet.

A pop-up art festival in Mumbai. Ira was supposed to be in town for a panel discussion. Aarav had work nearby.

They exchanged the idea over midnight messages.

Ira: "Let's meet. No pressure. Just as writers who orbit each other's minds."

Aarav: "Let's do it. Coffee, conversation, no filters."

But life, as always, had other plans.

Aarav's client presentation was rescheduled to the exact date. Ira's husband unexpectedly joined her on the Mumbai trip, wanting to "spend time" after weeks of distance.

They never said it aloud, but both felt the ache. That soft grief of something that could've happened but didn't.

Frequencies and Fate

The next night, they talked about vibrations.

Ira typed:

"Did you know every place has a frequency? You can feel the mood of a place before people speak. Some cities buzz fast; some hum slow. I think some people do that too."

Aarav replied:

"So what's mine?"

Ira sent:

"You? You feel like 432 Hz. Honest. Healing. Rare."

Aarav didn't know much about frequencies. But he knew that no one had ever described him like that before.

He sent her a playlist. Old-school rock, Hindustani instrumental, and that one Coke Studio song he never admitted he cried to.

She listened. And replied:

"You're not just a frequency. You're a soundscape."

"In a world of followers and filters, they had found each other's frequency. And for now... That was enough."

Chapter - 4

The Mirror Within

"Sometimes, even without speaking, we understand who still hears us."

Blue Ticks and Blank Screens

It's been three days.

That's how long Aarav stared at an empty inbox.

No new comment. No voice note. No new blog entry from @**baresoulletters.**

At first, he brushed it off. Life happens. But on day two, he typed a message and didn't send it.

"Everything okay?"

He deleted it.

He trusted her rhythm by now.

Still, he missed her voice. Not the sound, just the presence.

Ira - The Spinning World

At Ira's home, chaos danced in full volume. Guests had arrived from Jaipur and Delhi for her cousin's engagement, being hosted at their Pune bungalow, and Ira had become the unofficial event coordinator.

The living room was transformed with marigold garlands, chai counters, and aunties asking when she would have a baby. She smiled through it all gracefully, robotically.

Dressed in a green saree with jasmine flowers pinned into her neatly braided hair, she stood by her bedroom mirror as her mother peeked in with a tray of bangles. "Ira beta, please see if these go with your saree.

And check if Raghav's sherwani is ready!" she urged. Ira nodded politely, already ten minutes late for a Zoom call. Her phone pinged just as she opened her laptop.

A message from **@wildmind88:** "Hope everything's alright on your side of the sky.

Just checking in. No pressure." She read it three times, her heart softening with each one.

But with 17 unread family messages, a missed client call from London, and her blog deadline looming, she didn't have the energy to reply properly, not the way she wanted to.

So, she saved it. That night, lying in bed with mehndi still drying on her hands and her eyes stinging with fatigue, she whispered to herself, "He'll understand. He always does.

I'll write tomorrow." Because real bonds aren't broken by silence. They deepen in it.

Aarav - Unexpected Storms

It was supposed to be a slow week for Aarav.

Instead, his calendar exploded.

Three back-to-back presentations, an overnight system crash, and a new client that believed in 11 PM emails. By Thursday, his eyes were tired, his shoulders stiff, and his voice had taken on that clipped tone he hated.

The only thing he looked forward to each day was logging onto the portal. Reading @baresoulletters felt like soaking in a long, warm bath for his tired mind.

But for the first time in weeks, she hadn't posted in three days.

At first, he thought it was the app glitching. Then he checked again. Still nothing. No messages. No comments.

He tried not to spiral.

Maybe she was just busy. Maybe something came up. Life did that.

But still, he missed her.

Not in the frantic, addictive way.

In the quiet kind. The kind where your heart feels a little out of rhythm.

Aarav had his whirlwind.

A client had escalated a delivery deadline, his junior had quit mid-project, and his manager now expected him to "step up like a leader."

He skipped lunch. He didn't even get time to sleep. But what he didn't skip was checking that portal. Quietly. Like a ritual.

He didn't judge.

Didn't complain.

He just waited.

Aarav sat by his window the next evening, watching raindrops hit the glass like little stories trying to get in.

He could've messaged again. Could've called out into the silence.

But instead, he wrote.

"Sometimes, we disappear not because we don't care, but because life pulls too hard. And we return, not with guilt but with gratitude…for the ones who waited."

He hit send. Not expecting a reply. Just needing to say it.

And The Wait Is Over

Two days later, his phone vibrated at 10:41 PM.

Voice notes from @baresoulletters.

"Hey.

I've been completely hijacked by family chaos, work drama, and aggressive aunties with too many opinions.

I missed writing. I missed our little space here. And I missed your thoughts.

I hope you're still around because I've got like six things to rant about, and one of them includes how I almost cried over a forgotten charger."

Aarav smiled. Relief and warmth flood in together.

He replied with a voice note of his own:

"Still here. Still orbiting. And you're not allowed to cry over chargers anymore. Next time, I'm sending you a portable one. Or maybe just teleporting good energy."

Mirror Moments

That weekend, Ira finally opened her laptop. The engagement function was over. The relatives had left. Her mother-in-law was resting. Raghav was out for a business dinner.

She brewed coffee, lit a single lavender candle, and finally wrote again.

"When things get too noisy outside, I forget to hear myself. But some people stay, even in silence. To you, thank you for being that person."

Aarav commented:

"Some silences are sacred. Yours included."

They didn't talk much that day. But the silence felt held, not hollow.

The Cracks Beneath

Ira sat on her terrace that night. The air smelled of post-rain jasmine and burnt samosas. The city lights blinked tiredly.

She opened her journal and wrote:

"I don't know what this is between us.

But I know that when I think of 'safe,'

It's not a place or a person, it's a time.

10 p.m., when someone sees me without a filter."

Meanwhile, Aarav sat alone with his old diary again, flipping to a page he once wrote during college.

"I wonder if people like me are built to feel too much and say too little."

He smiled. And then added, beneath that line:

"Until someone shows up who hears even that."

Later that night, they didn't say much. They just sent songs. Random ones. Mood playlists. Lo-fi tracks with titles like “Moon and You” and “Things I Never Said.”

There was something comforting about knowing the connection didn’t need constant tending. It lived on, like coals under soft ash, ready to spark again at any moment.

“Not every bond is loud. Some grow in the quiet. In missed messages.

In unsent words. In the knowing… that someone still sees you. ”

“Real bonds aren’t broken by silence.
They deepen in it.”

Chapter - 5

Friction & Frequencies

"Sometimes the universe gives you what you asked for just to show you what you actually need."

Glitter Fatigue

Riya twirled in front of the mirror, holding up a pearl-studded lehenga.

"What do you think?" she asked Aarav. "It's from the latest runway drop. I can pull some strings and get it before the official launch."

Aarav, sitting on the edge of the bed, was checking his calendar.

"Looks good," he replied, tone neutral. He wasn't trying to be cold he was just tired.

Riya walked over and placed her manicured hand on his shoulder. “Babe, can you take me to the new rooftop bar this Saturday? Tanya’s throwing a pre-launch party. All our friends will be there. You’ll love it. ”

“I thought of taking a weekend off,” he said, finally looking up. “Like really off. Just nature, quiet, no Wi-Fi.”

Riya frowned like he’d just said he wanted to go live in a cave.

"You and this sudden obsession with disconnecting. It's honestly kind of a midlife crisis."

He gave her a half-smile.

"Maybe I'm just tired of conversations that sound like brand endorsements."

She laughed it off and walked away, humming a pop song.

Polished Parties, Unasked Questions

Meanwhile, at Ira's home, a soft jazz playlist played in the background as guests swirled glasses of wine and exchanged designer compliments.

Her husband, Raghav, had pulled out all the stops for their 5th anniversary: a rooftop dinner, a private chef, string lights, and crystal glassware.

Ira stood at the edge of the party, smiling and greeting guests while secretly checking her phone. Still no message from Aarav.

A woman from her husband's circle leaned in with a glass of Prosecco, voice coated in curiosity.

"So… any little ones on the way soon?"

Ira's face froze for a second before she smiled politely. "No plans. We're just… existing in the moment."

The woman gave a condescending chuckle.

"How very new-age of you."

Ira walked to the balcony, tuning out the crowd noise. A firework cracked in the sky, part of some nearby wedding celebration.

She took a deep breath. She missed her father in moments like this, the man who'd taught her to recognise real energy in a room. This one felt heavy. Hollow.

Belief Break

That night, she finally received a message from Aarav.

@wildmind88:

"Today felt like I was in a movie I didn't audition for."

She replied:

@baresoulletters:

"Same. Except mine was a social documentary in high heels."

Then she added:

"You ever wonder if we attracted our partners based on who we used to be?"

Aarav read the message twice. His response came slower this time.

"Maybe. Or maybe we were supposed to learn something through them before evolving."

Ira replied instantly:

"But if we've evolved and they haven't… then what?"

A long pause.

Aarav replied:

"Then maybe we start to feel lonely in a shared bed."

Ira left the chat unread for hours.

Something about the conversation unsettled her, not because he was wrong, but because he was right.

Frequencies that matter

The next evening, Ira finally replied." Do you believe we attract what we are? Or what we think we deserve?"

Aarav's message came quicker than usual:

"I used to think we attract our match in frequency. But now I think… sometimes we attract chaos just to understand peace."

Ira wasn't sure why, but she snapped back:

"So what are we now? A case study in spiritual upgrades?"

Aarav's message bubble showed "typing…" for a long time, then disappeared.

She stared at the screen. A lump rose in her throat.

Why did I say that? Why did that hurt him?

Ira started thinking and reading about the message she had sent: As humans, everyone is evolving at their own pace, and accordingly, they attract people around them.

Soft Recovery

Hours passed. No reply.

Ira finally sent:

"I'm sorry. I didn't mean it that way. I think I'm just overwhelmed."

Aarav replied shortly after:

"It's okay. I felt that too. We're both navigating noise."

A few moments later, another message came:

"Let's not let the noise kill the signal."

She smiled, tears prickling her eyes.

She sent a voice note:

"Thanks for holding space even when I get snappy. I guess it's easier to be patient with the world than with ourselves."

"Sometimes, the people we were drawn to once become mirrors of who we used to be. And sometimes, those we meet by accident reflect who we're still becoming."

Chapter - 6

Soft Places to Break

"Not all love stories are loud. Some unfold in whispers, where silence becomes a sanctuary."

Storms Settling Down

Aarav scrolled through his inbox absentmindedly, half-listening to the hum of the AC and the muffled sounds of Riya laughing on a video call in the other room.

The morning light filtered through Aarav's window in soft streaks, catching the rim of his coffee mug as he sat at his desk, half-awake, half-lost in thought. His inbox chimed with the familiar dull ring that usually signalled nothing more than a routine update, a policy circular, or a thread he was barely copied on.

But this one was different.

Subject: Pune Visit - Restructuring & Offsite Setup

Hi Aarav,

You've been assigned to lead the preliminary setup for our new Pune operations. Tentative travel dates for the coming week.

Let's discuss during the 4 PM check-in.

His cursor hovered over the mail for a moment, eyes tracing the words twice. Then a third time. Pune.

A slow breath escaped him; one he hadn't realised he was holding. The word didn't just mean geography anymore. It meant her.

The city had become a living postcard in his mind ever since their messages had begun gentle, layered, sometimes scattered like poetry in the margins of ordinary days. Ira was there. Living her life. Existing quietly, like the moon distant, yet always somehow present.

For a few seconds, the email felt less like a directive and more like a signal of an unexpected bend in the road.

He closed his laptop and leaned back in his chair, fingers interlaced behind his head. A strange blend of melancholy and excitement stirred inside him, like warm air meeting a cool breeze. It wasn't longing exactly, but something older than that. Something steadier. The quiet ache of something incomplete, now fluttering awake.

All day, he moved through meetings and spreadsheets with a secret tucked under his sleeve. He didn't rush. He didn't want to disturb whatever this was building into. The thought of seeing the same sky she did, breathing the same monsoon air that drifted across her window that was enough for now.

By the time the office hours drew to a close and the last calendar notification dimmed on his screen, Aarav opened his phone. His fingers hovered for a moment over her chat. Then, with a breath, he typed:

@wildmind88:

Seems like the winds are taking me your way. Office work restructuring off-site Pune.

Strange how life loops us back where the heart once paused.

No pressure to reply. Just thought you should know.

He stared at the message for a few seconds before pressing send.

And then he waited not just for her reply, but for the echo of something unnamed to return. Something he wasn't even sure he was ready for. Yet, somewhere inside him, he already knew:

Sometimes, the universe whispers in a beautiful way.

That evening, he messaged her:

"You won't believe this. The office is sending me to your city next week. Three days. Officially for numbers. Unofficially… maybe for magic?"

Ira's reply came with a voice note, laced with a grin he could practically hear:

"Okay, Universe. Now you're just flexing."

Wow, this Thursday!! (Only three days to go).

That's all that remained.

Ira reread his message "Seems like the winds are taking me your way…" and smiled without even realising it. Her thumb hovered over the screen, tracing the words like a secret she didn't want the world to see just yet.

He was coming. Not forever, not even for long, just a few days for work. But still, he was coming.

Her heart fluttered with a strange kind of calm, like the hush that follows the first rain. Something inside her felt watered, seen, quietly awakened.

She closed her laptop and leaned against the backrest of her chair, looking out toward the balcony where sunlight spilt lazily across the plants. The city was the same. The world hadn't changed. But everything felt different now.

In three days. She wanted to be ready. Present. Not half-listening to life.

She opened her calendar and, without hesitation, blocked those dates.

"On Leave – Work from Heart," she typed cheekily into her schedule and smiled.

She would take time off. Maybe not officially everywhere, but in the ways that mattered. She worked from home anyway she could stretch things, shift a few calls, draft blog posts late into the night if needed. What mattered was this: she wanted to be available. Not just in body, but in energy. For him.

For @wildmind88.

She didn't plan anything extravagant, just rearranged her heart's furniture to make space. Cleared her days gently like clearing a room before lighting incense.

Because when someone feels like home,

you tidy the corners before they arrive.

Even if it's just for a moment.

Welcome with Rain and Wildflowers

On a grey Tuesday morning, Pune greeted Aarav with a drizzle.

The rains had arrived quietly in Pune, as if the sky itself wanted to slow the world down for something soft to unfold.

Aarav sat in the backseat of the office car, watching raindrops race each other down the glass. The city blurred into watercolours, grey skies, honking rickshaws, chai tapirs with steaming flasks, and somewhere in between, a pulse of quiet anticipation inside him.

This time, it wasn't love.

It wasn't longing.

It was something in between an unspoken agreement of comfort. Of being understood without the weight of needing to explain.

And then, as the car slowed near the café they had agreed on, he saw her.

From the foggy pane, she looked like a scene half-painted, standing just under the awning, holding a deep blue umbrella. Her silhouette blurred slightly by the rain, yet unmistakably her. Curly hair damp with monsoon mist, a soft cotton kurta with hand-embroidered patterns, Lucknow, probably. Jhumkas that swayed gently as she turned her head. A dozen silver bangles stacked like stories around her wrist.

Aarav's lips curved, not into a smile, but something quieter. Familiar.

He stepped out slowly, waved off the driver, and said, "Go check into the lodge. I'll take the car from here."

The man looked at him, puzzled, then nodded and handed him the keys. Aarav got into the driver's seat, hands steady on the wheel, but before he could call her over, Ira was already walking toward the car.

She opened the passenger door and slipped in, folding her umbrella neatly. Rain still shimmered on her shoulders like little stars.

She looked at him, then tilted her head playfully.

"Well, Mr. @wildmind88, we finally meet."

Aarav chuckled a full, alive laugh that came from someplace deep. "And you must be Miss @baresoulletters."

They both laughed then, like old friends greeting the present moment rather than strangers discovering each other.

Ira asked, so can we please exchange names now!?

He introduced himself and shook hands, Ira found him warm, gentle and a strong individual. He asked: And yours?

She introduced herself loudly in her sweet voice. I am Ira. Aarav said: Ira, you mean Earth (Mother Earth) that nurtures. She smiled softly and said Yes and you, Mr. Calm, melodious sound. They both laughed.

Before he could say anything more, Ira looked at the steering wheel, then at him.

"Do you mind if I drive?" she asked, voice soft but sure.

Aarav didn't answer.

He just smiled, stepped out of the car, and walked around to the passenger seat without a word.

Sometimes, trust doesn't need permission. It just moves.

Ira played her favourite FM station in his car while driving 98.03 and they played a love song "Coming back to life".

They both looked at each other and smiled. It was the first time for Aarav to meet someone other than at work like that. He was gazing at her while Ira drove, thinking in his mind about his and Riya's first meeting and for him it was different. In an absolutely peaceful way.

Ira took him to a local café near the high street.

Aarav looked at her with his eyes sparkling.

"Welcome to my chaos," she said, handing him a filter coffee and a slice of banana walnut cake.

"Smells better than my apartment already," he smiled, feeling his chest loosen with ease.

They didn't hug. They didn't need to. The comfort hung in the air between them like a familiar blanket.

Later that afternoon, they drove toward a quiet dam outside the city that Ira used to visit with her father. The roads curved gently, surrounded by green hills, wildflowers, and the occasional temple bell echoing from afar.

As they walked along the dam's edge, she pointed toward the water.

"You know… I used to sit here as a kid and try to listen to the sound under the silence. Like the hum the Earth makes when it's not pretending to be loud."

Aarav looked at her, gently stunned.

"That's exactly what you are," he said. "The sound under the silence."

She smiled; the kind of smile that doesn't ask to be seen, just understood.

No Need to Perform

They sat by the dam, legs hanging over the ledge, sharing coconut chips and roasted peanuts from a brown paper cone.

No selfies. No check-ins.

Just stories. And pauses.

He told her about his mother's quiet strength and how he sometimes still heard her stitching clothes in his dreams.

She spoke about how cities left impressions on her skin, and how frequencies weren't just heard but.

Then silence. A long one.

And in that pause, there was no awkwardness. Just the kind of peace that came when someone accepted your pauses as part of your language.

A Soft Confession

As the sky began melting into a tangerine twilight, Aarav broke the silence.

"You know, we've been through weird waves. Ghost messages, snappy texts, life crashing in. But… we're still here."

Ira turned to him, voice barely a whisper.

" After all… we're sticking together. That matters."

Neither of them said anything after that.

They just watched the sky fade into soft lavender and let the wind speak for them.

The Unspoken Healing

That night, he walked her back to her society gate. Before leaving, she handed him a small notebook.

On the front: "Soft Places to Break. "

"It's empty," she said. "So you can start writing what you never had the space to."

He held it like it was fragile glass.

"I didn't know I needed this," he said, eyes glinting.

"That's how the best things arrive," she replied.

"Not every bond is built on declarations. Some are built on shared silences, on matching footsteps along a dam's curve."

Chapter - 7

Soul to Soul

"Not everything needs to be said. Some people become your healing, just by staying."

Gentle sunlight coming from the clouds makes its rays flicker in the.

Aarav texted Ira: Can we please again go to the same Dam? Where you took me yesterday, I will finish my work by 3 pm. And will catch up with you.

Ira: (replied with a smile)

Sure, I know you will like that place, coming from Mumbai. That place has my soul.

Aarav replied: "I can sense it. Let me know, where I pick you from?"

She replied: (with an emoji)

😇 Will you have tea at the tea stall near your office? I will be there.

Aarav checked her message and headed back to work to finish it all quickly.

The sky was bruised in a palette of muted pinks and greys as the evening settled around the dam. The breeze danced through the silence that often existed between Ira and Aarav, not heavy, not awkward, just… peaceful. It was the kind of silence that allowed your thoughts to rise gently, without judgment.

After a while, they meet …. They remember their chat about the tea stall and laughed out of happiness.

Ira filled up some tea in her thermos for a day, and they head for the location.

They sat on a boulder overlooking the slow current. The sound of water brushing against rocks felt like nature's version of exhaling. Ira sipped from her bottle of warm ginger tea, while Aarav absentmindedly traced a line in the dirt with a twig.

"Can I ask you something?" Ira finally broke the silence, her voice softer than usual.

Aarav glanced at her and nodded. "Always. "

"Did you ever… try reconnecting with Riya? I mean, beyond being civil, beyond going through the motions. Like… emotionally?"

Aarav took a long breath, then smiled faintly. "I tried. Once. I booked us a weekend trip, told her we could switch off phones and just be us. She said she'd come but brought her tablet and designer sketches anyway. We sat at the same table, but it felt like… opposite corners of the world."

Ira nodded slowly. "I asked Raghav if he ever missed the version of me from our early days. He said I've 'changed too much, 'and that maybe I need to be 'more grounded. 'But I think he meant less emotional, less spiritual, less me."

Aarav let out a soft, hollow laugh. "Riya once told me, 'You overthink everything. Just enjoy the moment. 'But how do you enjoy a moment that feels like a mask?"

There was a pause. The dam reflected a pair of birds skimming the surface, flying low, as if to listen in.

Ira spoke again, this time almost whispering. “Do you think they ever really saw us?”

Aarav turned to her. “I don’t think they ever knew who to look for.”

There was a quiet weight to that line. Ira rested her head back against the rock, closing her eyes.

“Sometimes,” she said, “I wonder if Raghav has ever asked himself why he wants children. Is it because he wants to nurture a soul? Or is it just the next checkbox after the anniversary party?”

Aarav tilted his head. “Do you think it’s that they lack emotional depth, or… that they were never taught to go deeper than appearances?”

Ira hesitated. “Maybe both. Or maybe they were just pampered in ways we weren’t. Maybe they never had to question anything because everything came easily. ”

“Comfort can make people numb,” Aarav said. “Riya’s life was built around being seen. Not felt. There’s a difference.”

A soft breeze lifted Ira’s hair across her face. Aarav reached out instinctively and tucked it gently behind her ear. It wasn’t romantic, it was reverent. Like acknowledging a truth, they both carried.

"Do you think we're being unfair?" Ira asked after a while. "To them, to ourselves? "

"We're being honest," Aarav replied. "Maybe for the first time in years."

They both leaned back now, staring at the sky as twilight settled fully around them.

"I used to think love meant fixing things," Ira murmured. "Fighting harder. Trying more. But now… I wonder if it's simply about being seen and heard without needing to ask."

Aarav looked at her, his voice low. "You don't have to ask with me."

And for the first time in years, neither of them felt alone in their truth.

They head to a city for dinner after witnessing a cloudy Sunset.

Chapter - 8

Unexpected Paths

"Not all who wander are lost — some are simply answering a call they didn't know they heard."

The restaurant was tucked away beneath a canopy of trees, fairy lights hanging like fireflies frozen mid-flight. Ira had suggested it "quiet, earthy, no noise, just music and good food." Aarav smiled. That sounded just like her. They sat across from each other, their plates mostly untouched, the conversation flowing more nourishing than the meal.

"You're not eating much," Ira said, twirling her fork slowly.

"I'm full on peace," Aarav replied, half-smiling.

After dinner, just as they stood to leave, a soft saxophone began playing in the corner. It was unannounced, unexpected. A warm jazz rhythm curled through the evening air like a memory returning.

Without thinking too much, Aarav looked at Ira, tilted his head slightly. "Dance?"

She raised an eyebrow but smiled. "It's not a ballroom."

He stepped closer, offering his hand, "Doesn't have to be. Just a moment."

She hesitated, then took his hand. And there, near the garden's edge, beneath the warm glow of amber bulbs and the scent of night jasmine, they swayed. Not choreographed. Not romantic. Just… human. Soulful.

No one watched. Or if they did, it didn't matter.

As the last note faded, Aarav reached into his coat pocket. A small white rose, its petals delicate, unassuming. He handed it to her wordlessly.

Ira looked at it for a moment before meeting his eyes. "No red?"

He chuckled. "White suits your aura. Calm. Clear. A little rebellious under the softness."

She didn't respond right away. Just held the rose close and smiled. That unspoken smile people share when their energy meets without words.

They walked back to her car in silence. The kind that spoke.

As they reached his hotel, she parked and turned toward him. For a moment, neither moved to say goodbye. It didn't feel like an ending.

Aarav turned toward the window briefly, then back to her.

"I have work tomorrow. Two more days here… then I go back."

She nodded. "I know."

Before he stepped out, Ira said softly, as if to the night,

"Tham ke rakha tha dil ko iss waqt ke liye. Shayad Jab darmiyaan jikr nahi bas jazbaat ho" (My heart was waiting for such a moment all this while, when there is no showing off, but just the presence). Aarav paused, then placed his palm gently on his heart. No words. Just resonance.

The car door closed softly behind him.

As Ira drove away, the white rose lay quietly beside her still, fragrant and alive. Just like this… unexpected path.

Chapter - 9

Hidden Wilderness

"In some other life, in some quiet sky, we already knew how to find each other."

The Next Day, Aarav finished his calls and walked into the cosy book café Ira had mentioned earlier, a quiet haven with mismatched floor cushions, walls of poetry, and the aroma of cinnamon coffee lingering like a memory. He found her sitting cross-legged near the window, a half-read Murakami resting in her lap, her hair tied in a loose bun that fell apart effortlessly.

She looked up and smiled, the kind of smile that felt like home after a long day.

"How was work?" she asked, sliding a steaming mug toward him.

"Manageable, but I kept thinking about that white rose," he grinned, settling beside her.

They sipped in silence before Ira leaned in, eyes gleaming.

"Tell me something wild," she whispered.

"Wild? "

"Yes. Your wildest dream holidays. No filters. No deadlines. Just you, and wherever your soul takes you."

Aarav paused for a heartbeat.

(Daydreaming while talking to Ira)

"Alright," he said. "We're in the Himalayas. Just you and me. No hotels, only tents. We trek through pine forests, cook simple meals over firewood, collect herbs, sleep under stars wrapped in layers and share warmth. You journal by candlelight. I sketch the sky. And somewhere, beside a mountain stream, we forget the world."

Ira closed her eyes, letting the vision form. "I can smell the cold air. I can feel the river mist. "

"We walk barefoot in grass wet with morning dew," Aarav continued. "We speak less, listen more. I think… I find my lost self there "

"And I discover the self I buried under expectations," Ira whispered. "And maybe… somewhere between the trek and the twilight, you kiss me."

Aarav held her gaze. "Wildly."

She nodded slowly. "Wild… and real."

They didn't realise when their hands found each other, or when their fingers intertwined like roots discovering shared soil. And in that dream, by a fire under a thousand stars, they kissed not in desperation, not to claim but to remember.

Then they stopped.

Aarav brushed her hair back, his voice steady but reverent.

"Our connections… are beyond bodies, Ira. I find myself in you."

Ira smiled through the glint of something sacred in her eyes.

"I feel the same. You reflect my soul without distortion."

Tell me something, Ira!! Have we met before?"

Ira was lost in her thoughts. He exclaimed and asked with a stare.

"Have we met before?"

Ira turned toward him.

"What do you mean?"

Aarav (eyes still on the water):

I mean… not in this life.

Somewhere else.

Another rhythm. Another time.

I don't know how to explain it, but being around you feels like finishing a sentence I didn't know I was writing."

He paused, then added:" Like déjà vu that feels too sacred to question."

Ira blinked slowly. Her lips parted, but not to speak. Her heart responded first.

Then she whispered,

"Maybe we promised each other to meet again…after we'd both forgotten what love is supposed to look like so we could recognise what it truly feels like."

Now they were sitting on a mat on a terrace of a cafe open to the sky.

The wind rose gently between them, carrying the scent of the city, a wild memory, and something unnamed.

For a few moments, they said nothing.

They just let the evening fold into itself, two souls breathing the same sky, as if remembering a song from a time when language didn't exist but love still did.

They hugged tight, slow, and soul-deep, no rush, no confusion.

In their imagination, they stood later at the mountain's edge, gazing at a river gliding through the jungle below. Silence was no longer empty. It was complete.

Chapter - 10

What Is Love?

"Somewhere between silence and sky, imagination writes what reality cannot."

A waiter leaned in, politely:

"Last order, ma'am?"

Ira blinked. So did Aarav.

They were back. Not in the mountains, but here. In this ordinary evening made extraordinary by presence.

"What is love, Aarav?" Ira asked, voice almost childlike.

He stirred his spoon slowly. "Not possession. Not roles. Maybe… just the freedom to be your whole self, and still be held gently."

Ira rested her chin on her palm. "Love, to me, is like a mirror. But it doesn't show your face, it shows your soul. And it says: I see you, even in your chaos."

They spoke. Hours passed. Lights dimmed.

"I believe," Aarav said, "what someone once said, 'You only meet, love, and care for someone as much as you love yourself.'"

Ira looked at him, stunned. "I believe the same. Everyone carries trauma, ghosts, broken versions of themselves. How we heal… without becoming a burden to others, that's how we grow. That's how we love."

The night slipped into cityscapes. The next day loomed. But it didn't matter.

As they walked by the riverside, Ira turned to Aarav.

"Your company is… completing. I don't know if I'll miss you. But after so long, I opened my heart again. That means something."

Aarav gently brushed her shoulder with his. “It means everything. ”

“We must meet again,” Ira whispered. “Maybe in your hometown. Uttar Pradesh. Maybe… we live that dream.”

At the car stand, she handed him a gift, a keychain, rustic yet soulful, tied with a note.

Aarav smiled as he waved goodbye. She didn’t say goodbye. Only, “Until next time.”

Return Journey

The next morning, Aarav sat in the car, fingers grazing the note.

“Key to your soul.”

He held the keychain crafted with a musical note, a mountain etched in metal, and his social media username engraved on the back. A gentle ache rose in his chest.

He reached home late.

Riya was in the kitchen.

She looked… calm. Different.

“I made brunch,” she said softly.

Aarav paused. “Everything alright?”

She nodded, looking up with glassy eyes. "I went through some of your old diaries. I didn't realise how deeply you think… how much you've given up for us."

Aarav stood frozen. Then slowly… a tear rolled down his cheek.

He hugged her.

Softly. Gently. Without guilt. Without expectation.

Not because everything was fixed but because, maybe, something had finally begun.

(Ira and Aarav)

They kept in touch, and they didn't need a portal post now to connect the frequencies. Somewhere, they were connected with an invisible bond.

"The world teaches us to be strong.

But sometimes, all we need …is somewhere soft to fall."

The journal Ira gifted Aarav became his companion.

He scribbled between meetings. On flights. In hotel lobbies. At midnight, silence returned like a loyal friend.

"I met someone who doesn't fix me, doesn't complète me …just lets me be whole in her presence."

Ira, too, wrote more. Her posts became layered, like inner conversations echoing out.

@baresoulletters:

"You can love someone and still feel lonely beside them.

But when someone notices the shift in your tone before you do …that's presence."

They spent that weekend offline.

Reading.

Watering Plant

Starting at thc skies

But in their hearts, a soft thread was tugging.

No pressure.

No labels.

Just a strange, gentle knowing:

We breathe easier when we're near each other.

Chapter - 11

The Real Self

Days passed, but something in Aarav remained quietly altered. He woke up earlier now. Started writing again. Picked up his old guitar, dusted off the silence inside him.

Riya noticed. She didn't say much. But she smiled more.

In Aarav's absence, Riya felt like understanding him more; she couldn't relate but could feel his agony.

She read in his book about his dreams and places to visit that wish list he created for himself. For her, it was all new and alien to live in a wood in a tent and cook by yourself! Riya thought of herself and chuckled: I'm not doing this somewhere away where there are no city lights glitter and fashion, & I'm cooking burnt food for Aarav. She smiled and came back to reality, and looked at herself in a mirror. She understood Aarav is doing a lot for the family, but now he has it all, and he should complete his "Wishlist" and write more often. (Riya finally understood the purpose of Aarav's dream)

He had seen tough times, and as his father said now, he had achieved a chair at the table with his hard work.

He called his parents that evening, and it was like little Aarav talking to his mother about his ambitions and dreams, and how he fulfilled them. They were really happy

Aarav scribbled his diary that night with poetry:

(A Soul's Whisper)

I wandered far to meet the world,
Wore every face that time unfurled,
A mask for joy, a smile for pain,
A thousand roles yet all in vain.

In silence deep, where echoes rest,
Beyond the noise, beyond the quest,
I heard a voice both soft and wise,
Not from the world but from inside.

Not built by gold, or shaped by name,
Not forged in pride, nor touched by fame,
It pulsed beneath each breath I drew
The part of me I never knew.

No mirrors showed this hidden light,
No map could chart its quiet flight,
Yet in the stillness, clear and true,
My soul said gently, "This is you."

Not perfect, no, but raw and whole,
A bruised but brightly burning soul,
The wounds I feared, the dreams I kept,
All led me home where truth had slept.

And now I walk, not to impress,
But barefoot in my humbleness,
No longer lost, no longer less
I live within… my real self's dress.

One Sunday morning, Aarav took a long bike ride to a quiet temple by the riverside. He sat on the steps, shoes off, sunlight warm on his back, watching birds glide across still waters.

He didn't need answers anymore. He only needed presence. And perhaps, a bit of courage to finally live as he truly was.

Far away, Ira stood in her garden with a cup of chamomile tea, barefoot on the dew-kissed grass. She had just finished her journaling. The pages were raw, brave, and real. Just like her.

She didn't chase validation anymore. She didn't shrink for comfort or pretend to fit into love she had long outgrown. She dressed for her soul now, long cotton skirts, a wild Bindi, mismatched earrings, and a heart at peace.

Raghav noticed the calm. Asked fewer questions. Maybe he didn't need to understand, only witness.

That week, they both found themselves texting again without attachment, but with openness.

Ira sent a picture of a pine cone she found in the city's only nature trail. Aarav replied with a photo of the temple steps and a one-line message:

"It's strange. I think I met myself after I met you."

She smiled and typed back:

"Maybe we were mirrors. Not to fall into but to reflect and return whole."

It feels like entering a portal.

One Month Later

In the mountains of Uttarakhand, two people stood beside a tent overlooking a valley. Same dream. This time, not imagined but lived.

The day wrapped in golden stillness.

The air was crisp but gentle, like a soft promise whispered by the mountains. Mist curled between the pine trees as if nature itself was exhaling slowly. Ira sat on the weathered wooden bench overlooking a quiet stream, her journal resting beside her, unopened. The pages had already said too much. Or maybe not enough.

She was tracing the rim of her terracotta tea cup grabbed at a local home stay. when she heard hurried footsteps behind her.

“You made it,” she smiled, not turning.

“ Of course I did.” Aarav’s voice was calmer than his breath, which was still catching up.

He slid onto the seat beside her, not too close, but not far either, just enough for their silences to intertwine.

Aarav:

“I wrapped the last frame early. Told my crew I needed to go chase the sunset.

They didn’t ask which one.”

He smiled, half amused, half transparent.

They sat there for a while, just watching the light dip gently across the hills, like a shy child peeking through drawn curtains.

Ira:

“You know… I’ve stopped explaining my silences to people.

But with you, they don’t feel like silence.

They feel like… presence."

Aarav didn't answer immediately. His eyes were fixed on the stream, the way it moved effortlessly around rocks without resistance. Then, softly, as if not sure whether he was speaking to her or something older, he exclaimed and asked with a stare.

"In case we forget who we are again," Ira said.

"Or how we found each other," Aarav added.

They carved a sentence into the wooden bench near the forest edge:

"We returned to ourselves here. Thank you, silence.":

Some places aren't vacations.

They're initiations.

They strip you. Ground you.

Remind you of what love looks like when no one is watching.

And sometimes, the wildest journey is the one that returns you home.

They cooked lentils over firewood, sang old folk songs, danced under stars, and sometimes just sat in silence as the wind wrote poems around them.

Ira looked into his eyes and asked softly,

"If we had met earlier… would you have fallen in love with me? Would you have married me?"

Aarav smiled with a quiet ache in his eyes.

"I would have loved to… with all my heart."

She tilted her head gently. "Then why not?"

He exhaled slowly, as if releasing a truth he'd carried for lifetimes.

"Because I want to stay in love with you… not just live through the idea of it."

"Sometimes, marriage comes with roles, expectations, and slow fading… what we share now it's untouched, free, real. And I want it to stay that way… forever."

No labels. No future-talk. Just this being seen, being known.

One cold evening, Aarav looked at Ira across the fire and said:

"I used to think love was about finding someone to hold onto.

Now I know it's about finding someone who reminds you to hold onto yourself."

Ira reached for his hand. "You reminded me that I can be wild and still be whole."

They didn't kiss this time. They didn't need to.

They watched the sun set behind snow-capped peaks, wrapped in woollen shawls, heartbeats syncing to the rhythm of the wilderness.

The sun filtered softly through the tall deodars as Ira and Aarav sat on a fallen log, silence cocooning them like an old friend. A gentle breeze played with the leaves, whispering truths neither of them dared to say aloud.

They talked about their childhoods.

She told him how her father once made her identify constellations in army tents.

He told her how he used to sleep better when his mother read to him in dim yellow light.

They weren't just two adults anymore. They were two kids remembering how to feel safe.

The woods echoed with silence again, but it was deeper now, rich with unspoken understanding. They didn't need to hold hands. The stillness between them was its form of closeness.

The other day,

The pine-scented air was gentle, cradling the quiet between them. Ira and Aarav sat beneath a sprawling deodar tree, its roots anchoring them like the truths they'd come to accept in silence. The sun poured softly through the leaves, painting golden patterns on their faces. It had been hours since they spoke, yet their presence was louder than any conversation.

Suddenly, a rustle caught their attention. A wild mountain dog, hairy, rugged, and adorably untamed, appeared from between the trees. Its golden-brown fur shimmered slightly in the sun, and its eyes held a kind of purity no words could capture.

Ira's face lit up; a glow even brighter than the sunlight. "Oh! Look at him, Aarav," she whispered, "I've always loved animals… dogs especially. They're such honest souls. I feel like I understand them more than people sometimes."

Aarav turned to her; his expression thoughtful. "You're an empath," he said gently, watching the dog settle in the distance as if it belonged to this shared moment. "Empaths… they connect deeply with animals, with nature. They feel things unspoken. They understand broken souls not out of sympathy, but because they carry fragments of that brokenness within themselves too."

Ira looked at him, wide-eyed and soft. "Is that what this is? Why do I feel so drawn to everything raw and unpolished?"

Aarav nodded, smiling. “Yes. That’s your real self-speaking.”

As the sun climbed higher, they gathered themselves and walked back to their tent, pitched further up the slope, secluded, a little wild like the dog, and perfect. The noon air was crisp as they unpacked the vegetables they’d bought from a local mountain vendor: fresh carrots, soft potatoes, beans, herbs, and a tin full of freshly collected cow’s Milk.

Aarav insisted on helping. “No hierarchy here,” he chuckled, “we cook this together.”

While Ira arranged things outside the tent, gently peeling and chopping, Aarav wandered into the nearby woods, collecting dry twigs and branches for the evening campfire. Ira watched him from a distance, how easily he blended into the natural rhythm, how peaceful he looked among trees and silence.

“He’s a man of the forest,” she whispered to herself. “And maybe… I’m more like him than I ever allowed myself to be.”

By evening, the meal was simple but nourishing: creamy mashed potatoes with lightly sautéed carrots and beans, sliced local fruits, and warm ginger tea in metal mugs. They ate slowly, feet buried in earth, faces lit by the mellow hues of the dying sun.

As night unfurled its cold arms, they changed into their warm clothing. Ira requested a moment alone in the tent to change. Aarav stepped out respectfully. But through the delicate, almost-transparent tent window, he caught a glimpse, just a fraction of her silhouette, her long hair cascading down, a dress sliding off her shoulder. His gaze immediately dropped. He looked away, whispering to himself, “She is beautiful… but I will protect her dignity. This space is sacred.”

Later, they sat side by side near the fire, now glowing in soft orange hues. Ira strummed her ukulele, the melody floating between them like smoke. They sang, laughed, and read fragments of poetry, some hers, some his, all shared. Their voices, their hearts, no longer guarded.

A full moon reflected in the water body just beyond them, framed by towering deodars. It was the kind of view that made time pause. Aarav turned to look at Ira and, in her eyes, he saw something more than affection. He saw a mirror. A reflection of his real self. His twin flames.

Overcome with feeling, Ira wrapped her arms around him. Tight. Like a hug that remembered lifetimes. Aarav hugged back, neither needing to explain nor question it. They didn’t kiss. But their fingers laced together, tighter than ever, as if this moment was the last breath of something sacred.

The fire dimmed. The air grew colder. Stars scattered across the sky, and a comet brushed past like a blessing.

Ira rested her head on Aarav's shoulder. Her breathing slowed. He realised she had drifted off. He didn't move. When he was sure she was fast asleep, he gently carried her to the tent, placed her under the thick blankets, brushed a strand of hair from her forehead, and kissed it lightly.

"I see you," he whispered. "All of you."

Then he stepped to his side of the tent and lay in silence, listening to her breath… steady, real, nearby.

Tomorrow, they would return to their separate worlds.

But tonight, they had met their real selves.

When they parted again, it wasn't goodbye.

It was space for life, for healing, for truth.

Ira continued her spiritual workshops, journaling with a green pen and wrote a book titled "The Real Self."

Aarav moved back to his hometown, started a community library and opened a soulful café named "Wilderness Within."

They stayed in touch. Not out of habit, but resonance.

And sometimes on quiet nights, they'd each find themselves staring at the same moon, whispering:

"What if love is just… finally meeting yourself?"

Love isn't always about forever.

Sometimes, love is about finally remembering who you are.

One night, Aarav posted:

📸 **@wildmind88**

A photo of a half-bloomed Gul mohar tree.

Caption:

"Healing isn't always loud.

Sometimes, it's in washing your coffee mug,

Choosing to take the stairs,

Saying 'no 'without guilt.

You won't always be applauded.

But you'll feel your breath come back."

Ira smiled as she read it.

She didn't comment.

Instead, she went and took out her old harmonium, touched the keys that hadn't felt her fingers in three years.

Music flowed. Just for her.

One day, Aarav and Ira met again, this time by accident.

Both were attending a common friend's book launch in Delhi.

She spotted him across the room.

He turned just as she looked.

Their eyes locked.

The hug was soft. Familiar.

They didn't talk about the past.

They didn't ask about what's next.

Instead, they walked to a quiet spot outside.

Aarav took a deep breath. "Do you ever wonder what this was?"

Ira replied,

"I think it was a portal."

He smiled. "To what?"

She looked at him—soft, knowing.

"To the real us."

They sat on a bench under the moonlight. No hands held.

Just two people who had journeyed through ache, reflection, and silence

And had found the one thing they'd been searching for all along:

Themselve

Maybe love isn't always about forever with someone else.

Maybe it's about returning to the real self you buried beneath expectations, roles, and noise.

And maybe…
The deepest love story is the one where you finally meet yourself.

Epilogue

Returning from the hills felt surreal.

The traffic was back. Emails blinked. Calendars filled. The silence they had breathed in now seemed distant but not lost.

Because something within them had shifted permanently.

Aarav returned to Riya, who greeted him with a designer scarf and photos from a brand collab.

"How was it? "she asked.

He smiled. ".Quiet"

She nodded, already scrolling through her phone.

Ira walked into her home. Raghav was watching a documentary on luxury real estate.

"Did you get what you needed? "he asked casually.

"I think I got what I'd forgotten, "she said, softly.

They didn't label it. They never needed to. There was no grand closure, no last-minute confession, no dramatic turning point.

And yet, something had shifted quietly, irrevocably.

In a world that rushed for answers, they had chosen pauses.

In a world obsessed with love stories, they had discovered something softer: The reflection.

Aarav returned to Mumbai changed not by her presence, but by his own awakening.

Ira remained in Pune, not waiting, not wishing, just walking lighter.

The notebook she gifted him was half-filled now. With verses. With truths. With silence made visible.

Sometimes, you don't cross paths to end up together.

Sometimes, you meet to return to yourself.

They still wrote. Not every day. Not in the same way. But sometimes, when the moon was right and the silence deep enough, they would share a post an old melody, a new metaphor, a pause.

Just a thread between two frequencies that once met in perfect resonance.

And maybe, that's all love ever needed to be. (Until we meet again)